Love From,
Allison and

From
Eddie

The Egg and The Eye

THE ART OF EGG COOKERY
AROUND THE WORLD

By ESTHER LEWIN AND
BIRDINA LEWIN
ILLUSTRATED BY JAY RIVKIN

ALSO BY ESTHER LEWIN, BIRDINA LEWIN AND JAY RIVKIN:

STEWED TO THE GILLS: *Fish and Wine Cookery*

RICE 'N' EASY: *A Complete Rice Cookbook*

THE WOMEN'S LIB COOKBOOK *or Whose Place Is In The Kitchen?*

THE MEN'S LIB COOKBOOK *or Feel Free*

GROWING FOOD • GROWING UP: *A Child's Natural Food Book*

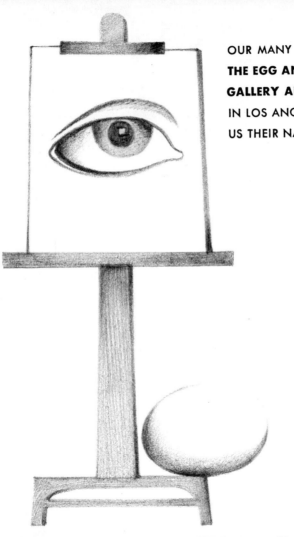

OUR MANY THANKS TO
**THE EGG AND THE EYE
GALLERY AND RESTAURANT**
IN LOS ANGELES FOR LENDING
US THEIR NAME.

TABLE OF CONTENTS

**PRIMARY COLORS:
YELLOW AND WHITE** ■ 9
Basic Preparations

ALL IT'S CRACKED UP TO BE ■ 21
Breakfast

WHICH CAME FIRST? ■ 35
Appetizers and
First Courses

**ALL YOUR EGGS
IN ONE BASKET** ■ 47
Lunch, Dinner,
Late Supper

PALATABLE EGGS ■ 67
Accompaniments

EGG ON ■ 87
Sandwiches

**THE WORLD IN
AN EGGSHELL** ■ 99
Desserts

MASTERPIECES ■ 119
Baking

INDEX ■ 131

THE EGG AND THE EYE

Which came first? The palette egg or the palate egg? The reds and yellows of Russian Orthodox Easter eggs or the reds of Huevos Rancheros and the yellows of Hollandaise? The portraits painted with egg-tempera or the platters of Eggs Benedict? The finely chiseled egg of marble or the shimmering freshly peeled hard-boiled egg? Is the polychromatic painting of a golden sunrise more or less artistic than the vision of two golden sunny-side up eggs. Does the fragile pastel-hued confectioner's egg with its show viewed through a tiny peep-hole bring more delight than a caramel custard? Will China best be remembered for carved ivory eggs or Egg Flower Soup? Is there a similarity between a surrealistic egg painting and egg salad? When making a collage of egg shells, can deviled eggs be far behind? Is the painting "Concert In The Egg" by Hieronymos Bosch more a symphony than a Mousse au Chocolat? Beauty is in the eye of the beholder . . . and the pot holder.

Primary Colors: Yellow and White

BASIC PREPARATIONS

9

SOFT BOILED EGGS 1

Bring water (enough to cover eggs) in a saucepan to a heavy boil. Gently lower eggs one at a time on a spoon into water. Boil eggs for 3½ minutes. Remove eggs with a spoon and run under cold water for a few seconds. This stops the cooking process. Put in an egg cup and remove top with an egg cutter or knife. Season with salt and pepper.

SOFT BOILED EGGS 2

Put eggs in a sauce pan and cover with cold water. Bring water to a boil, reduce heat slightly, and time 2 minutes for a perfect soft boiled egg. Serve as above.

Cooking a perfect soft boiled egg is an art.

POACHED EGGS

Fill shallow pan two-thirds full of boiling salted water or water to which you have added one-half teaspoon white vinegar. Break each egg into a saucer and carefully slip into water, which should cover the eggs. Do not allow water to boil after eggs are added. When there is a film over top and white is firm, remove to rounds of buttered toast. Serve plain or with a sauce. Use egg poacher if preferred. Poached eggs may be made ahead of time. When eggs are done, remove from hot water and drop into a bowl of ice water. Cover immediately and refrigerate up to 3 days. To use, place drained eggs into hot simmering water for 3 minutes. Drain and use as freshly poached.

Viva La Egg!

FRIED EGGS

Break eggs into a skillet containing a little butter or margarine and cook over low heat until eggs are set. Or when eggs begin to set on bottom, add 1 teaspoon water, cover tightly and cook until desired doneness. This gives a delicate egg that has the appearance of a poached egg. Eggs over easy are fried eggs turned when bottom is set. Do not overcook.

Keep your sunny-side up—or down over easy.

SCRAMBLED EGGS

There are as many ways to scramble eggs as there are cooks. Some cooks say cook eggs slowly over low heat; others say to do them quickly over a high heat. One cook will say only use butter, another cook says margarine is just as good. Another insists on either bacon or ham drippings. There are experts who add thick cream, others who swear by half and half, some who advocate skim milk, some add water, and some add nothing at all. While the eggs are frying, some cooks stir them constantly, some only once or twice, some flip the eggs only once. When it comes to scrambling eggs, we're with Humpty Dumpty, right on the fence.

Experiment yourself and find the way to scramble eggs that suits your taste best. Scrambled eggs are delicious just plain, but you can vary them by adding a tablespoon of capers or one teaspoon finely chopped chives and parsley. Another variation is 2 green onions sliced and one-quarter chopped green pepper or grated cheese scrambled with the eggs.

Pop art?

HARD-BOILED EGGS

Put eggs in a saucepan. Cover eggs with cold water and bring to a boil. This keeps the yolk in the center. Boil for 20 minutes. Rinse eggs in cold water until cool. Use right away or store in refrigerator unshelled.

The all time picnic favorite—dining al fresco.

SHIRRED EGGS

Eggs are prepared by breaking each egg into buttered custard cups or casseroles and baking in a 350 degree oven until the eggs are set to desired doneness. The seasoning is sprinkled over the top of the eggs when done.

A baked egg.

CODDLED EGGS 1

Bring a pan of water to a rolling boil. Put eggs in the water and turn off the heat. Cover the pan. In 20 minutes the eggs will be ready to eat—with firm whites and soft yolks.

CODDLED EGGS 2

If you have covered egg-coddling cups, butter inside of cup and break egg into cup. Screw on lid. Place cups in a pan of water. Bring water to a boil, reduce heat and simmer 12-15 minutes. Remove from water. Remove lids and serve eggs in cups.

Cooking an egg with T.L.C.

BROILED EGGS

Melt butter or margarine in skillet; when hot, slip in eggs one by one. Cook the bottom of eggs to desired doneness, then place pan under broiler and cook eggs until soft, medium or hard as desired. Season.

VARIATIONS:

Add ¼ to ½ cup of cream to butter before putting eggs in skillet.

Sprinkle each egg with ½ teaspoon favorite cheese before slipping under broiler.

Really firm sunny side-up eggs.

OMELETTE

> 3 tablespoons butter or margarine
> 8 eggs
> 2 tablespoons half and half
> ¼ teaspoon salt
>   dash pepper

Melt butter in a large frying pan. Beat eggs, half and half, salt, and pepper. Put into pan and cook slowly until eggs are set, lifting edges of omelette so that the uncooked eggs can run under cooked eggs. When eggs are done, slip omelette onto a large platter and fold over in half. If you like your omelette drier, put pan under a hot broiler for 30-40 seconds until the top starts to brown. This is a puffier omelette, too. Serves 4.

VARIATIONS:

Cheese Omelette: Add 4 or 5 slices of American, Old English, or cheddar cheese to eggs just after you put them in pan. Cheese will melt as eggs cook.

Fines Herbes: Add 2 or 3 teaspoons combined of all or each of the following dried or fresh herbs such as parsley, chervil, dill, sweet basil, tarragon, chives.

Mushroom: Make omelette as above. Make mushroom filling

by slicing one half pound mushrooms thin, seasoning with salt and pepper and sauteing in butter or margarine until tender. Add one tablespoon sherry, 2 tablespoons hot water and a dash or 2 of Maggi seasoning. Slip omelette onto serving platter. Put mushrooms over half of omelette and fold other half over mushrooms.

Chicken Liver: Before making omelette, saute ¾ pound chicken livers and one small onion, sliced thin in 4 tablespoons butter or margarine. Season with salt and freshly ground black pepper. Saute quickly so that livers do not overcook. Add 2 tablespoons sherry or rose wine, 2 tablespoons hot water (enough to make a little sauce). Make omelette and put on serving platter. Spoon chicken livers and sauce over half of omelette and fold omelette over livers.

Spanish Omelette: Before making omelette, saute one small onion, sliced thin, one stalk celery, diced, half a green pepper, sliced thin, one clove garlic, minced, in butter or margarine until almost golden. Add one 8 oz. can tomato sauce, ¼ teaspoon salt, ⅛ teaspoon pepper, ¼ teaspoon sweet basil, ¼ teaspoon seasoning salt, 2 dashes Tabasco sauce. Simmer for 15 minutes. Make omelette and fill as above.

Leftovers: Almost any leftover that has a sauce will make a good omelette. For instance shrimp in either cream sauce or creole sauce, sweet and sour pork, chicken a la king, ham in cherry sauce . . .

All It's Cracked Up To Be

BREAKFAST

HAM AND EGG CAKE

6 eggs
1 tablespoon instant or granular flour
½ teaspoon salt
½ cup milk
1 tablespoon butter or margarine
½ lb. ham, thinly sliced
chopped parsley

Beat eggs lightly with flour and salt. Slowly add milk. Melt butter in an iron or very heavy skillet. Pour eggs into skillet and reduce heat to the lowest possible setting. It may be necessary to place an asbestos pad under the skillet if heat isn't low enough. Cook 20 minutes until eggs are set in a custard. Cut each ham slice into 3 long strips and pan fry quickly until curled and brown. Cover finished eggs with ham strips and sprinkle with parsley. Serve immediately from skillet. Serves 4.

Egg custard for breakfast.

BACON AND CHEESE SOUFFLE

  6 thin slices bread
1/3 lb. cheese, sliced or grated
3/4 teaspoon salt
1/4 teaspoon mustard
1/4 teaspoon paprika
  5 eggs beaten
  2 cups milk
  6 bacon strips

Arrange bread and cheese in layers in buttered casserole beginning and ending with bread. Mix milk, eggs and seasonings and pour over bread and cheese. Lay bacon over top. Cook in a 350 degree oven until puffy and a knife inserted in center comes out clean, about 45 to 60 minutes. Serves 6.

Create a souffle in layers—an easy high-living idea.

EGGS AND ONIONS

1 large onion, chopped fine
6 tablespoons butter or margarine
8 eggs
4 tablespoons milk or half and half
¼ teaspoon salt
⅛ teaspoon pepper

Saute the onions in 3 tablespoons butter over medium heat for exactly 10 minutes. Stir occasionally. Beat the eggs, milk, salt, and pepper. When the onions are ready, add rest of butter. Pour eggs over onions and scramble the eggs until they are done. Serves 4.

A traditional Sunday morning breakfast from the kibbutz.

SALAMI AND EGGS

8-12 slices Kosher salami
2 tablespoons butter or margarine
8 eggs
4 tablespoons milk or half and half

Lay the salami on the bottom of a large frying pan so that slices do not overlap. Fry over medium heat until salami is cooked and starts to brown. Add butter to pan. Beat eggs and milk together and pour over salami. Cook eggs either omelette or scrambled style. Serve immediately. Serves 4.

A delicious deli breakfast.

EGGS SHOYU

2 green onions, sliced
3 tablespoons butter or margarine
6 eggs
2 teaspoons shoyu, Japanese soy sauce
1 tablespoon mirin or sake

Cook onions in butter in a frying pan for one or 2 minutes until onions begin to wilt. Beat eggs, shoyu, and mirin and add to pan and cook until eggs are set. Scramble eggs lightly. Serve on hot rice or toast. Serves 3.

Japanese eggs made in the U.S.A.

HUEVOS LISBOA

- 1 tablespoon vegetable oil
- 1 onion, chopped
- 2 boneless pork chops, diced
- 1 ½ inch thick slice of ham, diced
- 1 tablespoon instant or granular flour
- ½ cup hot beef bouillon or consomme
- ½ teaspoon salt
- ¼ teaspoon pepper
- 1 large tomato, chopped
- 8 eggs

Heat oil in heavy skillet. Add onion, pork, and ham and cook until very brown. Stir in flour. Add bouillon. Cook and stir until well blended. Add salt, pepper, and tomato. Cook until very thick. Pour into an open, oven-proof dish and break the eggs over the top. Bake in a 350 degree oven until the whites have set. Serves 4.

Portuguese ham 'n eggs.

HUEVOS RANCHEROS

2 8 oz. cans tomato sauce
1 4 oz. can green chili salsa
6 eggs
½ lb. Jack cheese, cut in strips
6 corn tortillas

Mix tomato sauce and chili salsa. If you like a milder sauce, use half the amount of salsa. Put sauce in a large skillet and simmer for 10 minutes. Break eggs one at a time into a saucer and slip them carefully into the sauce. Cover and poach eggs over low heat until eggs are almost set. Cover eggs with cheese and cook until cheese is melted. While eggs are cooking, heat tortillas in oven until warm. To serve, put a tortilla on a plate, carefully spoon an egg out of the sauce and place on tortilla. Spoon sauce over egg and tortilla. Serves 6.

Ole! That's what the Mexican chicken said.

HASH AND EGGS

2 large cans corned beef hash
1 onion, grated
½ cup catsup
6 eggs

Mix corned beef hash, onion, and catsup. Put into a shallow greased baking pan. Make 6 indentations with the back of a spoon. Break an egg into each hole. Bake in a 350 degree oven for 20 minutes or until eggs are set. Serves 6.

A way out Western way for breakfast.

EGGS BENEDICT

4 eggs
2 English muffins
4 thin slices ham or Canadian bacon
Hollandaise Sauce (page 81)

Poach the eggs. While eggs are cooking, toast the English muffins. Put a half muffin on a plate. Lay a slice of ham on each muffin. Put a poached egg on the ham and cover all with Hollandaise Sauce. Serve immediately. Serves 4.

Pretty as a picture.

EGGS BASQUE

4 large green peppers
4 eggs
  salt and pepper
1 cup tomato sauce

Parboil peppers 5 minutes. Drain, cut off stem ends, remove seeds and membrane. Place each pepper in a buttered cup, cut end up. Drop an egg in each pepper and season with salt and pepper. Place cups in pan of hot water, and bake in a 350 degree oven until eggs are set, about 5 to 10 minutes. Serve with tomato sauce. Garnish with ham or bacon.

A nice huevo with eggs.

FRENCH TOAST

4 eggs
¼ cup milk or half and half
¼ teaspoon salt
4 slices white or egg bread
   butter or margarine
   powdered sugar
   jelly or syrup

Beat eggs with milk and salt and pour into a shallow bowl or pan. Soak bread in eggs, turning occasionally, for 15 minutes. Fry on both sides in butter until golden brown. Cut in half in triangles. Sprinkle lightly with powdered sugar. Serve with jelly or syrup. Serves 4.

For a sweet change, soak the bread in egg nog (leave out the liquor) and then fry in butter.

*In New Orleans, this is called Pain Perdu—
another way to use leftover bread.*

MATZO BREI

8 eggs
¼ cup water
8 matzos
1 teaspoon salt
¼ teaspoon pepper
¼ teaspoon onion salt
4 tablespoons nyafat, butter, or margarine

Beat eggs and water in a large bowl. Hold each matzo under hot running tap water until matzo starts to get soggy. Break up the matzos into pieces about 2 inches square and put them into the bowl with the eggs. Add salt, pepper, and onion salt and mix. Soak them for 20 minutes. Heat a large frying pan and melt the nyafat. Add the matzos including any leftover egg. Fry over medium heat until matzos are lightly browned. Turn and fry the other side. Cook the matzos in one big pancake or break the matzos into 3 inch pieces as they fry. Sprinkle with sugar or jelly or serve with sour cream and lox. Serves 4.

Mastering an old art.

Which Came First?

APPETIZERS AND FIRST COURSES

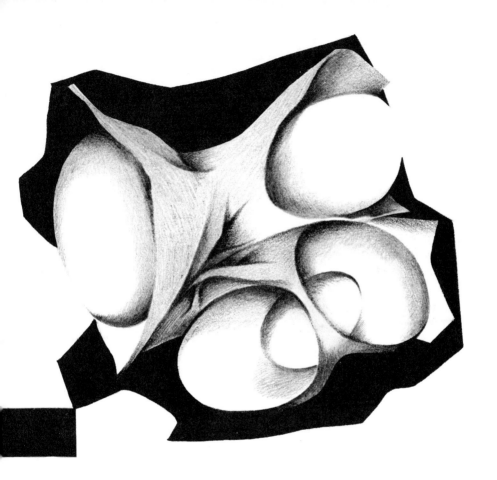

PICKLED EGGS

12-16 hard-boiled eggs
2 cups cider vinegar
2 tablespoons sugar
1 teaspoon salt
4 peppercorns
1 clove
¼ teaspoon celery seed
¼ teaspoon powdered ginger
1 clove garlic

Add seasonings and spices to vinegar (dilute ⅓ with water if strong) and simmer 8 minutes. Put eggs in a bowl that has a tight lid. Strain brine and pour over the eggs. Cover and let stand two days before using. A sprig of dill, a few caraway seeds, or onions are other flavors that may be added to the brine to give a special flavor.

Spicy Vorspeisse.

DEVILED EGGS

12 hard-boiled eggs
2 tablespoons mayonnaise
1½ teaspoons mustard
¼ teaspoon onion salt
1 teaspoon Worcestershire sauce
salt
pepper
paprika

Cut hard-boiled eggs in half lengthwise. Remove yolks and mash. Add mayonnaise, dry mustard, onion salt, and Worcestershire sauce. Mix well. Add salt and pepper to taste. Pile yolk mixture into egg whites. Sprinkle with paprika. You may garnish top with chopped chives, parsley or caviar. Other seasonings such as onion juice, caviar, anchovies, ham, sardines, cheese may be added to the yolk mixture. Serves 12.

To be eaten indoors or outdoors—a moveable feast!

CHEESE PUFFS

¼ cup butter
½ cup boiling water
⅓ cup flour
½ cup grated Parmesan cheese
¼ teaspoon salt
2 eggs

Heat butter and water until butter melts; then add flour all at once. Stir until smooth. Remove from fire, add cheese and salt. Beat. Beat eggs in, one at a time. Drop from tip of teaspoon on a greased cooky sheet. Bake 35 to 40 minutes in a 350 degree oven. Cool. Cut off tops. Fill bottom with egg salad filling (page 88). Replace tops.

Egg salad putting on airs.

QUENELLES

    2 lbs. fillet of halibut, poached in clam juice
    2 tablespoons butter or margarine
    3 tablespoons instant or granular flour
    ½ cup hot clam juice, reserved from cooking
    1 teaspoon salt
    ½ teaspoon white pepper
    2 eggs, separated

Put fish through finest blade of meat grinder. Set aside. Melt butter, stir in flour and gradually add hot clam juice and seasoning. Stir constantly until very thick and paste-like. Remove from fire. Beat in egg yolks. Add ground fish. Beat egg whites very stiff and fold into mixture. Form into tiny balls. Moisten hands in cold water between rollings. Place in a steamer over hot water until they are thoroughly heated and cooked—about 10 to 15 minutes. Serve with toothpicks as appetizers. Serve with hot Hollandaise sauce. (page 81).

Fish balls to go with highballs.

FRIED MOZZARELLA

mozzarella cheese
flour
egg, beaten
dry bread crumbs
oil for frying
coarse salt (Kosher)

Cut mozzarella in strips about ½ inch thick and 3 inches long.
Roll them in flour. Dip in egg. Roll in bread crumbs and fry in
one-half inch oil in a skillet (preferably electric). Proportions
vary and these can be just a few pieces or dozens of pieces de-
pending on your needs. Cook quickly, just until cheese begins
to show. Drain on paper towels. Sprinkle lightly with coarse
salt and serve immediately.

Gooey, but good. Pass napkins.

INDIVIDUAL QUICHE LORRAINE

1 pkg. pie crust mix
6 thin slices Gruyere cheese, diced
6 slices of bacon, broiled crisp and crumbled
3 eggs
1 tablespoon instant or granular flour
½ teaspoon salt
  cayenne
1 tablespoon melted butter or margarine
1½ cups half and half

Prepare pie crust mix according to directions on package. Roll out very thin and cut into twelve 3" circles. Turn 2 cup cake pans upside down. Press circles of dough over pans to make shells. Bake in a 400 degree oven for 10 minutes. Remove from oven and reduce heat to 375 degrees. Carefully remove shells from pans and place on a cookie sheet. Divide cheese and bacon into the 12 shells evenly. Beat eggs, add flour, salt and cayenne. Stir in butter and add the half and half. Pour custard into the shells. Place cookie sheet in oven and bake 40 minutes or until custard is set. Serve warm.

Miniatures.

EGG SALAD ASPIC

1 tablespoon gelatin
2 tablespoons cold water
2 cups hot vegetable-clam juice
8 deviled egg halves (page 37)
¼ lb. tiny bay shrimp
1 cup chopped celery
2 green onions, sliced
watercress

Soften gelatin in cold water, then dissolve in the hot juice. Pour a quarter inch layer of stock in bottom of a ring mold. When slightly set, carefully place deviled eggs yolk side down in the aspic. Refrigerate to set. When the remaining aspic begins to thicken, add shrimp, celery, and onions and mix well. Pour over the eggs. Chill to set. Unmold on watercress. Serve with Piquant Dressing. Serves 4.

Calypso dish—sure to please.
Pretty for appetite to tease.

PIQUANT DRESSING

1 tablespoon watercress leaves, chopped
1 tablespoon chopped parsley
½-1 teaspoon minced onion
1 tablespoon prepared mustard
¼ teaspoon pepper
¾ teaspoon salt
2 hard cooked yolks, sieved
¾ cup oil
¼ cup vinegar

Mix greens, onion and seasonings, and make a paste with the sieved yolks; add oil gradually. When all are mixed add vinegar gradually. May be made in blender.

GOLDEN CUBE GARNISH FOR CLEAR SOUP

3 egg yolks
1 whole egg
½ cup beef broth
½ teaspoon salt
dash cayenne
dash nutmeg

Beat eggs, broth and seasonings. Pour into a buttered pan. Set pan in hot water to a depth of one quarter to one half inch. Bake in a 350 degree oven until firm, about 25 minutes. Cut in dice or fancy shapes. Serve one to 2 tablespoons for each serving of clear soup such as chicken broth.

Soup to serve in your best eggshell china.

EGG FLOWER SOUP

  4 cups chicken broth
  2 teaspoons soy sauce
½ teaspoon MSG
  2 tablespoons diced celery
  1 green onion, sliced thin
  2 sprigs chopped watercress
  1 egg, beaten

Heat soup and all ingredients except egg until soup starts to boil. Lower heat and very, very slowly add egg to soup in a thin stream. Stir soup constantly as egg breaks up and cooks. Serve immediately. Serves 4.

A dainty dish to set before a Ming.

All Your Eggs In One Basket

LUNCH, DINNER, LATE SUPPER

NEST EGGS

1 package frozen chopped spinach
4 large frozen artichoke bottoms
½ teaspoon salt
3 tablespoons sour cream, room temperature
4 eggs poached
1 cup Blender Hollandaise (page 83)

Cook spinach according to directions on package. Drain almost dry. Set aside in a warm place. Cook artichoke bottoms according to directions on package. Drain well. Set aside in a warm place. Poach eggs. Combine spinach with salt and sour cream. Spread on a warm serving dish. Make dents to hold artichoke bottoms. Place poached eggs in artichoke bottoms. Cover with hollandaise. Serve immediately. Serves 4.

A picturesque lunch in the garden.

WEST INDIES CASSEROLE

     2 tablespoons butter or margarine
    ½ lb. crabmeat
     1 cup frozen petit pois, thawed
     4 poached eggs
       pepper
     1 can cream of shrimp soup
       paprika

Heat butter in a casserole or skillet that can be placed in the oven. Cook the crabmeat until very hot. Remove from heat, scatter peas over the crabmeat. Place poached eggs on top. Sprinkle with pepper. Cover with undiluted shrimp soup. Sprinkle with paprika. Bake in a 350 degree oven for 10 minutes. Serve immediately. Serves 4.

A duty free import from France.

SPECIAL STRATA

6 slices firm white bread, crusts removed
1 can, undiluted cheddar cheese soup
3 eggs, beaten
1½ cups milk
1 teaspoon salt
½ teaspoon white pepper
¼ teaspoon paprika

Cut bread slices in quarters. Arrange a layer of bread in a deep buttered casserole. Spread bread with some cheese soup. Repeat until all the bread and soup are used. Combine all the other ingredients. Pour into casserole. Cover lightly and chill for at least 3 hours. Bake in a 400 degree oven for 45 minutes or until puffed and custard is set. Serve immediately. Serves 4.

A modern dish made more modern.

CREAMED EGGS MONTREAL

 1 package frozen asparagus spears
 6 hard-boiled eggs, sliced
 1 can cream of asparagus soup diluted with
½ can half and half
 1 can French fried onions
   salt
   white pepper
 3 tablespoons grated Parmesan cheese

Cook asparagus according to directions on package. Drain well. Butter a small casserole and place alternate layers of egg slices, soup and onions and ending with soup. Arrange asparagus spears across the top. Sprinkle lightly with salt and pepper. Cover with Parmesan cheese. Bake in a 350 degree oven for 15 minutes. Serves 4.

A dejeuner in the life of a Canadian.

EGGS A LA KING

        6 hard-boiled eggs
        4 tablespoons butter or margarine
        4 tablespoons flour
    1½ cups milk
        1 3 oz. can sliced mushrooms, drained
        1 tablespoon pimiento, chopped
      ¼ teaspoon salt
      ½ teaspoon seasoning salt
      ¼ teaspoon celery salt
      ⅛ teaspoon pepper
          dash Tabasco sauce
          chopped parsley

Melt butter, add flour and stir until smooth. Add cold milk. Cook and stir constantly until thick. Remove from fire and place over hot water. Add mushrooms, pimientos, seasonings and eggs cut in quarters lengthwise. Heat thoroughly. Serve on toast or patty shells. Sprinkle with parsley. Serves 3.

Fit for a queen, too.

CHICKEN MOUSSELINE

6 uncooked chicken breasts, boned
4 eggs
½ onion, grated
1 tablespoon lemon juice
1⅓ cups thick cream
1 teaspoon salt
¼ teaspoon white pepper
dash cayenne

Put chicken through food grinder twice. Beat in eggs one at a time, stirring until mixture is blended. Add onion, lemon juice, cream, and seasonings. Pour into a buttered casserole and bake in a 350 degree oven for 30 minutes. Serve with Blender Hollandaise Sauce (page 83). Serves 6.

A luncheon at the Palais D'Art.

ARTICHOKE BOBATIE

8 canned artichoke bottoms, drained
8 large mushrooms, chopped
1 small onion, chopped fine
2 tablespoons butter or margarine
¼ teaspoon salt
   dash pepper
2 cups cooked rice
3 tablespoons mayonnaise
1 10½ oz. can cheddar cheese soup
4 eggs beaten
¼ teaspoon salt
   dash pepper

Saute onion in butter until brown. Add mushrooms, salt, and pepper, and more butter if necessary and saute until done. Mix rice and mayonnaise lightly. Spread in shallow buttered pan. Make 8 indentations in rice. Place artichoke bottoms in rice so that they are almost buried. Stuff artichokes with mushroom and onion mixture. Put soup in a bowl and heat with a fork until light and smooth. Add eggs, salt, and pepper. Gently pour over rice so as not to disturb mushroom stuffing. Bake in a 350 degree oven for 40 minutes or until knife inserted comes out clean. Serves 4.

A version of the native African custard dish.

SKILLET CORN

8 slices bacon, diced
2 onions, sliced thin
2 tablespoons diced red pepper
   fresh corn cut from 8 ears
½ teaspoon salt
8 eggs, slightly beaten
   dash pepper

Fry bacon crisp and drain off half of the fat. Add onions and red pepper and saute until light brown. Add corn, salt, and pepper and cook 5 minutes. Add eggs and cook until set, stirring up from bottom of skillet. This may be served on toast. Canned corn, drained, may be substituted. Sharp cheese grated or cubed may be stirred in at the end just long enough for it to melt. Serves 4.

From pre-Colombian pots—scrambled corn off the cob.

POTATO AND ONION OMELETTE

2 potatoes, cut in ½ inch cubes
1 onion, chopped
4 tablespoons butter or margarine
½ teaspoon salt
½ teaspoon caraway seeds
½ teaspoon juniper berries (optional)
8 eggs
2 tablespoons half and half
4 tablespoons butter or margarine
6 heaping tablespoons sour cream

In a large skillet fry potatoes and onions in 4 tablespoons butter over medium heat until potatoes are tender and brown. Add salt, caraway seeds, and juniper berries. Beat eggs with half and half. Melt remaining butter in a large frying pan. Add eggs and cook until set. Slip onto a large serving platter. Put potatoes and onions on half of omelette. Gently fold. Spoon sour cream over omelette and serve immediately. Serves 4.

A down to earth omelette.

EGGS BOMBAY

8 eggs, poached
2 tablespoons butter or margarine
2 teaspoons curry powder
1 egg yolk
3 cups hot rice
1½ tablespoons flour
1 cup chicken broth
2 tablespoons heavy cream

Melt butter and add flour and curry powder, stirring to blend thoroughly. Add broth and stir until slightly thickened. Remove from fire and stir in yolk mixed with the cream. To serve, arrange poached eggs on a warm platter covered with rice. Cover with curry sauce. Garnish with red ginger and chopped green onions. Serves 4.

Curry favor with flavorful eggs.

ZUCCHINI FRITTATA

2 medium size zucchini, diced
3 tablespoons fresh bread crumbs
3 tablespoons half and half
3 tablespoons grated Parmesan cheese
½ teaspoon salt
¼ teaspoon white pepper
4 eggs, beaten
2 tablespoons butter or margarine

Parboil diced zucchini just until barely tender. Drain well and press out any excess moisture with a clean cotton towel. Soak bread crumbs in half and half for five minutes. Combine all ingredients except eggs and butter. Stir eggs into zucchini mixture. Melt butter in a heavy skillet. Pour in egg mixture, reduce heat, and cook for 3 minutes. When bottom is set (lift corner with a spatula to test) place skillet under the broiler flame for about 30 seconds. Cut into wedges. Serves 4.

A pancake comes to dinner.

MEAT LOAF
WITH HARD-BOILED EGGS

1 onion, chopped
2 tablespoons butter or margarine
3 slices white bread, crusts removed
1½ cups hot milk
1 lb. lean ground beef
½ lb. lean ground pork
½ lb. lean ground veal
1 teaspoon salt
½ teaspoon pepper
¼ teaspoon allspice
4 hard-boiled eggs, shelled

Saute onion in butter. Set aside. Tear bread into pieces and soak in hot milk for 1 hour. When bread and milk are custard-y, combine all ingredients except eggs in a large bowl and mix thoroughly. Grease a 9″ loaf pan. Spread half the mixture on the bottom. Place the eggs, end to end, in a row down the center. Cover with remaining meat. Bake in a 325 degree oven for one hour. Pour off any excess fluid. Unmold on a platter. Serve in slices. There will be a slice of cooked egg in the center of each serving. Serves 6.

An egg hunt all year 'round.   **59**

KEDGEREE

1 cup flaked cooked fish
1 cup cooked rice
4 hard-boiled eggs, quartered
   dash of cayenne pepper
¼ teaspoon or more curry powder
   salt
1 10½ oz. can cream of mushroom soup
¼ teaspoon grated ginger

Mix flaked fish, rice and eggs. Add seasonings to taste and two-thirds can of soup mix. Put into buttered casserole. Mix ginger with remaining soup and spread over casserole. Bake in a 350 degree oven for 30 minutes. Serves 4.

A typical Capetown fish casserole.

EGG FOO YUNG

6 eggs, well beaten
½ cup chicken or any cold meat, chopped
1 1 lb. can bean sprouts, drained
½ cup chopped celery
1 tablespoon chopped green pepper
½ cup shredded green onions
¼ teaspoon salt
oil

Combine vegetables and meat. Add salt and eggs, beat well. Drop from large spoon (to make a cake one-half inch thick) into one-half inch hot oil. Cook until brown on both sides. Drain on paper towel. Serve hot with Foo Yung Sauce. Serves 4 to 5.

FOO YUNG SAUCE

½ cup water
½ teaspoon cornstarch
1 tablespoon soy sauce
dash MSG
1 tablespoon sherry

Mix 2 tablespoons water and cornstarch to make a smooth mixture. Add remaining water. Add soy sauce, MSG and cook until sauce is thickened and clear. Add sherry.

Fortune cookie says: Eat at home.

CHILIS RELLENOS

8 canned green chili peppers (3 or 4 cans)	4 eggs, separated
½ lb. Jack cheese	4 tablespoons flour
	oil

Beat egg yolks slightly. Add flour and mix. Fold in stiffly beaten egg whites. Spread the chilis out flat. Cut the cheese into one and a half inch pieces. Put a piece of cheese in the center of each chili and fold so that cheese is held by the chili pepper. Heat one and a half inches oil in a skillet. Place a heaping tablespoon of the batter in the moderately hot fat. Put one chili pepper in the center and cover immediately with another tablespoon of the batter. Fry until golden brown on both sides. Do this in several batches. Serve with Sauce Caliente. Serves 4.

SAUCE CALIENTE

½ onion, minced	1½ teaspoons salt
1 clove garlic minced	¼ teaspoon pepper
2 tablespoons oil	2 cups tomato puree
2 cups boiling water	1½ teaspoons oregano
2 beef or chicken bouillon cubes	

Saute onion and garlic in oil until brown. Dissolve bouillon cubes in water and add to onions. Add rest of ingredients and simmer for 15 minutes.

Hot eggs!

CHEESE SOUFFLE

        4 tablespoons butter or margarine
        4 tablespoons flour
    1½ cups milk
        1 teaspoon salt
          dash cayenne
          dash dry mustard
        1 cup grated sharp American cheese
        6 eggs, separated

Preheat oven to 350 degrees. Melt butter, add flour, then milk, making a thick white sauce. Add seasoning and cheese and stir until cheese is melted. Beat in the egg yolks. Cool. Fold in stiffly beaten whites. Pour into a souffle dish. Bake for 25 minutes or until set. Serve immediately. You may vary the souffle by adding one cup well drained chopped cooked spinach or cooked and mashed eggplant (seasoned with grated onion). Or you may add one cup flaked crab or cooked fish or one-half cup ground or finely chopped ham. Make the addition to the white sauce before adding egg yolks. Serves 4 to 6.

Good impressionists!

CHUTNEY OMELETTE

8 eggs
3 tablespoons half and half
  salt
4 heaping tablespoons chutney
¼ teaspoon curry powder
4 tablespoons butter or margarine
4 tablespoons sour cream
4 teaspoons chopped toasted walnuts or cashews

Beat eggs with half and half, chutney, curry, and generous sprinkling of salt. Melt butter in a frying pan and add eggs. Cook over moderate heat until omelette is set. Slip omelette onto serving plate. Fold in half and spoon sour cream over omelette. Sprinkle with chopped nuts. Serves 4.

A Delhi omelette.

APPLE PANCAKE

1 cup flour, sifted
½ teaspoon salt
½ teaspoon baking powder
3 teaspoons powdered sugar
1½ cups milk
4 eggs
2 large tart applies
  lemon juice
4 tablespoons butter

Sift together first 4 ingredients. Stir in milk and beat until smooth. Add eggs, one at a time and beat hard. Peel and core apples, slice very fine and sprinkle slices with lemon juice. Heat 2 tablespoons butter in a large heavy skillet. Pour in batter and arrange apple slices on top. Cook for a few minutes. Heat oven to 350 degrees. Butter a large baking pan with remaining butter and turn contents of skillet over onto the pan. Bake until top is golden brown. Serve immediately with sugar and cinnamon. Serves 2.

Fun cookin' pfannkuchen.

Palatable Eggs

ACCOMPANIMENTS

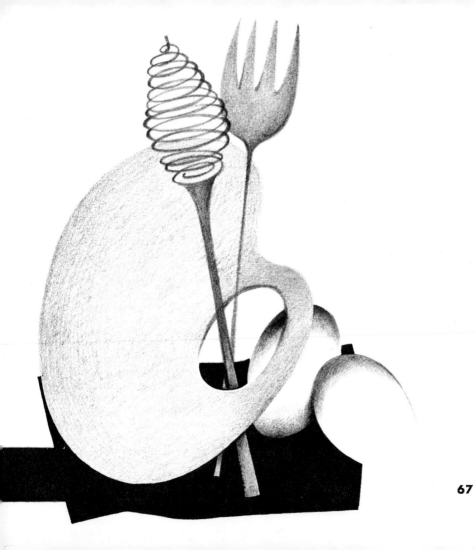

SPAETZLE

4 eggs, beaten
1 cup flour
½ teaspoon salt

Combine eggs, flour and salt. Beat well. If batter seems thin, place in refrigerator for an hour. Bring a large pot of salted water to a rolling boil. Spread the batter out thin on a dinner plate. With a teaspoon, push small amounts of batter from the edge of the plate into the boiling water. Keep pushing the batter toward the outer edge of the plate. Spaetzle will rise to the top of pot when they are ready. Test one with a fork for tenderness before removing from pan. Drain well. Serve with butter, salt and paprika.

Free form dumplings.

GNOCCHI

2 cups warm, unseasoned mashed potatoes
1 cup warm Pate A Choux (page 129)
  salt
  pepper

Combine all ingredients and beat well. Add salt and pepper to taste. Fill a large buttered skillet with about 1½ inches salted water. Bring water to a boil then reduce to a very low simmer. Drop small rounded spoonfulls of batter into the barely moving water. Cover pan and cook until gnocchi rise to the top of the water. Drain well and serve with butter and Parmesan cheese, or a flavorful tomato sauce.

Italian dumplings . . . in the style of Botticelli.

EGG DUMPLINGS

1 cup flour
1 cup farina
3 teaspoons baking powder
4 teaspoons cold butter or margarine, cut in pieces
½ onion, grated
3 eggs, beaten
⅓ cup milk
1 teaspoon salt

Combine first 4 ingredients with your fingertips until they look like coarse meal. Beat in the onion and eggs. Add milk and salt and beat until smooth. Bring a large pot of salted water to a rolling boil. Drop large spoonfulls of batter into the water. Do about 6 dumplings at a time. Reduce heat and cook until they rise to the top of the water. Remove from pot with a slotted spoon. Keep in a warm place and repeat until all are cooked. Serve warm with butter or with chicken or meat gravy.

Large hearty dumplings for iconoclasts.

MATZO BALLS

      6 eggs
        water
      1 lb. matzo meal
      3 tablespoons soft chicken fat
    1½ teaspoons salt

Beat eggs until light and foamy. Add 2 half egg shells of luke-warm water. Beat in all the remaining ingredients. Mixture should be fairly loose. If it seems too stiff add a little more warm water. Cover lightly and place in the refrigerator for several hours to become firm. To prepare, bring a large pot of salted water to a full rolling boil. Reduce heat slightly. Moisten hands with cold water and make matzo balls about 1½ to 2 inches in diameter. Drop them in the water as you form them. Do not roll them all and then drop in the water. They will rise to the top of the water when ready. Drain well. Serve in Chicken soup. Leftovers can be cut in half and heated with chicken or brisket gravy. Or they may be sliced and sauteed in butter or margarine as an accompaniment to meat.

Matzo balls in chicken soup . . . a cure-all for everything.

NOODLE RING

2 cups fine noodles
4 eggs, separated
2 tablespoons water or milk
½ teaspoon paprika
½ teaspoon onion powder
¼ teaspoon white pepper
1 teaspoon salt
1 cup heavy cream, whipped

Boil noodles in salted water. Rinse with cold water. Stir in yolks, water or milk and seasoning. Fold stiffly beaten egg whites and whipped cream together and fold into noodles. Pour into a greased 9 inch ring, set in pan of hot water. Bake in a 350 degree oven until firm, one hour or longer. Unmold on a round serving platter. Serves 10-12.

Molded ring to serve plain or fill center with creamed chicken or shrimp and surround noodles with petit pois.

POTATO PUFFS

6 medium size baking potatoes
¼ teaspoon salt
¼ teaspoon onion powder
1 recipe Pate a Choux (page 129)
   oil for frying

Bake potatoes. Remove from shells and mash thoroughly with seasonings. Combine potatoes with warm Pate A Choux. Place in refrigerator to become firm. Pour oil to a depth of 3 inches in a deep saucepan. Heat to 375 degrees. Dust hands with flour and roll about a teaspoon full of dough in a small ball and drop into oil. Turn with a slotted spoon until they become golden. Do not crowd the pan by frying too many at a time. Keep warm in the oven on a paper towel lined cookie sheet.

Alpine delicacy . . . the lowly potato reaches new heights.

ASPARAGUS PUDDING

1 package frozen asparagus cuts
¼ cup butter or margarine
1 cup coarse cracker crumbs
¼ teaspoon dried parsley
½ teaspoon grated onion
½ teaspoon salt
¼ teaspoon white pepper
2 cups milk, heated
2 eggs, slightly beaten
  paprika

Cook asparagus according to directions on package. Drain well. Melt butter and cook cracker crumbs, parsley, onion, salt and pepper for a few minutes. Pour milk into eggs slowly, stirring constantly. Add crumb mixture and asparagus. Pour into a buttered 9" loaf pan. Bake in a 375 degree oven for 35 minutes. Let rest in pan about 5 minutes before unmolding on serving platter. Dust with paprika and serve in slices. Serves 4-6.

Cubist pudding with asparagus.

FRITO MISTO

Batter

1¾ cups flour, sifted
2 teaspoons salt
½ teaspoon white pepper
1 cup warm water
½ cup vegetable oil

3 egg whites
vegetables
salt
oil for frying

Beat first 5 ingredients in electric blender at high speed for 30 seconds. Pour batter into bowl and let rest 2 hours. Just before using the batter, beat egg whites stiff and fold into batter.

Vegetables

raw carrot sticks
raw cauliflower, broken into small flowers
small fresh mushroom caps
asparagus stalks, parboiled and dried
raw zucchini spears

Method

Sprinkle vegetables with salt. Pour vegetable oil to a depth of 3 inches in a small deep saucepan and heat to 375 degrees. Dip vegetables in batter, coat well, lift out with tongs, drain off any excess batter and drop into oil. Fry a few minutes until golden. Drain and serve immediately. These can be kept warm on a paper-lined cookie sheet in the oven, but they are better if served immediately.

Italian Tempura.

CORN-CHEESE ESCALLOP

4-6 ears corn (3-4 cups scraped)
4 eggs, beaten
1 cup grated cheese
1 teaspoon salt
⅛ teaspoon nutmeg
  dash cayenne
  sour cream

Mix all ingredients except sour cream and place in a buttered baking dish. Set in pan surrounded by hot water. Bake in a 325 degree oven until mixture is set and slightly browned on top, about 20-30 minutes. Serve from baking dish. Put a heaping tablespoon of sour cream on each serving. Serves 6.

Gold the Conquistadores left behind.

ESCALLOPED SPINACH

2 eggs, well beaten
2 cups milk
2 cups cracker crumbs
4 tablespoons melted butter
¾ teaspoon salt
   dash pepper
2 cups cooked chopped spinach, drained
1 onion, chopped fine

Mix all ingredients thoroughly, reserving a small amount of crumbs and about one tablespoon melted butter. Place in a well-greased casserole and cover with the crumbs and remaining butter. Bake in a 325 degree oven until crumbs are browned and mixture is set in center, about 35 minutes. Serves 4.

Spring mood captured in a casserole.

CARROT SOUFFLE

3 tablespoons butter
3 tablespoons flour
1 cup milk
3 eggs, separated
4 cooked sieved carrots
    salt, paprika, pepper, powdered ginger

Melt butter in a saucepan, add flour and mix. Add milk and cook until thickened. Stir in carrots. Stir in yolks. Add seasonings to taste. Cool, then fold in stiffly beaten whites. Pour in greased casserole or souffle dish that has been buttered on the bottom only. Set in hot water and bake in a 350 degree oven about 30 minutes, until firm and delicately brown. Garnish with parsley. Serves 6.

4 carrots make this a gem of a dish.

LETTUCE SALAD
WITH CREAM

3 hard-boiled yolks
1/3 cup cream
1/4 teaspoon salt
white pepper
1/2 teaspoon sugar
2 tablespoons lemon juice
salad greens

Sieve yolks; add remaining ingredients in order given. Add more salt if necessary. Pour over salad greens and toss lightly.

An idea hatched in Brussels.

ONION CAKE

1 package hot roll mix
1 egg, beaten
1 tablespoon soft butter or margarine
4 large onions, sliced
1/3 cup butter or margarine
2 cups sour cream
3 eggs
1/2 teaspoon coarse (Kosher) salt
1/2 teaspoon caraway seeds

Prepare hot roll mix according to package directions but before beating all of the flour into the yeast mixture beat in one beaten egg and one tablespoon soft butter. While dough is rising, saute onions in the 1/3 cup of butter until they are limp and golden. Cool. Beat the 3 eggs and the sour cream until well blended. Add the onion mixture. When dough has doubled in volume, punch down and let rest about 10 minutes. Roll out into a rectangle slightly larger than a 9" x 13" pan. Butter the pan and press the dough into the pan, bringing it up to an inch edge on all sides. Pour onion filling into dough. Sprinkle with coarse salt and caraway seeds. Bake in a 350 degree oven for 1 hour. Serve warm cut in squares. Serves 12.

A connoisseur knows his onions.

HOLLANDAISE SAUCE

  1 tablespoon boiling water
  1 tablespoon lemon juice
  ¼ teaspoon salt
  ⅛ teaspoon white pepper
    dash cayenne
  3 egg yolks
  8 tablespoons softened butter or margarine

In the top of a double boiler, over hot, but not boiling water, mix one tablespoon boiling water, lemon juice, salt, pepper and cayenne. With a wire whisk, beat in the egg yolks and one quarter of the butter. Beat until butter is melted and sauce begins to thicken. Add the second quarter of the butter and continue beating in the same manner. Repeat with the third and last quarter of butter. Remove from heat for a few minutes, beating constantly. Return to hot water and whisk a few more times. Add a few drops of lemon juice and whisk again. If at any time, the sauce separates or shows signs of curdling, add one or 2 tablespoons cold water and continue beating until sauce is smooth.

Original French.

EASY HOLLANDAISE

6 egg yolks, beaten slightly
2 cups cream
½ teaspoon salt
4 tablespoons lemon juice

Beat yolks and cream, then add lemon juice and salt. Cook in double boiler over warm water until thick, stirring constantly. Serve on cooked vegetables. Yield: 2 cups.

Translated from the French.

BLENDER HOLLANDAISE

    2 whole eggs
    2 tablespoons lemon juice
      dash of cayenne
  ½ teaspoon salt
  ½ cup soft butter or margarine
  ½ cup boiling water

Put all ingredients, except water, in blender. Turn blender on high speed and very gradually add water. Blend for 30 seconds. Put sauce into top of double boiler and cook over hot, but not boiling, water, stirring constantly until sauce thickens. If sauce separates when heated, beat in 2 tablespoons boiling water, a drop at a time.

French abbreviation.

MAYONNAISE

3 egg yolks, room temperature
½ teaspoon dry mustard
¾ teaspoon salt
   dash white pepper
   dash cayenne
2½ cups olive oil, room temperature
1 tablespoon lemon juice
2 tablespoons boiling water

Put egg yolks, mustard, salt, pepper, cayenne, and a few drops lemon juice into a bowl and mix with a whisk. Add the oil drop by drop until you've used 1 cup oil and the sauce begins to thicken, beating constantly. Then in a very slow thin trickle, beating constantly, add the rest of the oil. Occasionally thin mayonnaise with some of the lemon juice. Use up all the oil and lemon juice. Then add the boiling water whisking briskly. Makes 2½ cups.

French original.

BLENDER MAYONNAISE

1 egg
½ teaspoon dry mustard
1 teaspoon salt
dash white pepper
dash cayenne
1 teaspoon sugar
1½ cups salad oil
3 tablespoons lemon juice

Put egg, mustard, salt, pepper, cayenne, sugar and three-quarters of a cup of oil in blender. Blend at high speed until thoroughly combined. Add half the remaining oil in a thin stream with blender running at high speed. Add lemon juice and blend. Add remaining oil and blend until thick. Stop and start blender to stir down sauce. Makes one and three-quarter cups. If you have different instructions for your own blender, use them.

French copy.

Egg On
SANDWICHES

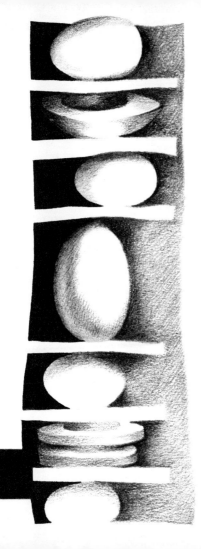

EGG SALAD SANDWICHES

Egg Filling 1

4 hard-boiled eggs
1 green onion, minced
  mayonnaise

salt
pepper

Chop eggs and add onion and enough mayonnaise to bind. Add salt and pepper to taste.

Egg Filling 2

4 hard-boiled eggs
⅓ cup chopped cooked bacon
  or

⅓ cup chopped stuffed olives
3 drops Worcestershire sauce
  cream or mayonnaise

Chop eggs, add bacon or olives and Worcestershire sauce. Add enough cream or mayonnaise to give a spreading consistency.

Egg Filling 3

4 hard-boiled eggs
½ cup chopped watercress or parsley
½ teaspoon salt

lemon juice
pepper

Chop eggs and add water cress. Add salt, lemon juice and pepper to taste.

Three egg salads: Tri one try them all.

FRIED SANDWICHES

2 eggs, beaten
1 cup milk
½ cup flour
½ teaspoon salt
  dash pepper
  sandwiches, such as deviled ham, cheese, salami or chicken,
  crusts removed, cut in diamonds, quarters or rounds
  butter or margarine for frying

Mix eggs, milk, flour, salt and pepper. Dip sandwich in batter and fry until nicely browned on both sides. Serve at luncheon or tea with several on a plate accompanied by small bunch of grapes and few large strawberries dusted with powdered sugar.

How to make a good sandwich batter.

SOUFFLED CHEESE SANDWICH

6 slices bread
3 eggs, separated
½ teaspoon salt
⅛ teaspoon pepper
¼ teaspoon paprika
1 cup sharp grated cheese

Remove crusts and toast bread on one side. Beat whites until stiff. Season yolks and beat until light. Fold yolks and grated cheese into whites. Pile on untoasted side of bread slices. Place on a buttered cookie sheet and bake in a 350 degree oven about 10 minutes until puffy and brown. Serves 6.

A cheese sandwich with a new image.

MONTE CRISTO SANDWICH

8 slices white sandwich bread
  butter or margarine
4 slices turkey
4 slices ham
4 slices yellow or white brick cheese
2 eggs, beaten
1 cup milk
½ cup flour
½ teaspoon salt
  dash pepper
  butter or margarine
  powdered sugar
  currant or strawberry jelly

Spread both sides of bread with butter. Make 4 sandwiches using a slice of turkey, ham, and cheese on each. Make a batter with the eggs, milk, flour, salt, and pepper. Cut each sandwich in half. Dip each piece completely in the batter and fry in butter until golden brown on each side. Sprinkle lightly with powdered sugar and serve with jelly. Serves 4.

A very American after the show favorite.

DENVER SANDWICH

3 eggs
2 tablespoons milk
½ cup small-diced ham
½ cup diced green pepper
2 green onions, sliced
1 tablespoon chopped pimiento
3 tablespoons butter or margarine
8 slices white toast
　mayonnaise, butter or margarine

Beat eggs and add milk, ham, green pepper, onions and pimiento. Melt butter in a frying pan. When butter is bubbling, add egg mixture. Cook until bottom is set. Cut omelette in 4 pieces and turn to cook other side. Spread toast with mayonnaise or butter. Put piece of omelette on 4 pieces of toast. Cover with rest of toast. Serves 4.

Hot lunch from the range.

EGG SMORREBROD

4 slices white or egg bread
   butter or margarine
2 hard-boiled eggs, sliced
4 large thin onion slices
1 2 oz. can anchovies, drained
   dill weed

Spread butter generously on each slice of bread. Place a slice of onion on each slice of bread. Arrange the egg slices on the onions. Sprinkle with dill weed. Divide the anchovies over the eggs. Makes 4 sandwiches.

Three dimensional sandwich.

EGG AND CAVIAR

4 hard-boiled eggs
2 tablespoons red caviar
1 teaspoon grated onion
1 tablespoon mayonnaise
4 small slices slices pumpernickel bread

Chop eggs. Add caviar, onion and mayonnaise. Add more mayonnaise if necessary to bind eggs and caviar. Heap on pumpernickel bread. If you use large slices, cut into quarters. Serve open face. Serves 4.

An egg collage.

EGG AND OLIVE
AND BACON

4 hard-boiled eggs
½ 4½ oz. can chopped ripe olives
4 slices bacon, cooked crisp
1 tablespoon mayonnaise
8 slices cracked or whole wheat bread

Chop eggs. Add olives, crumbled bacon, and mayonnaise and mix well. Add more mayonnaise if necessary to bind mixture. Spread on 4 slices bread and close sandwiches with rest of bread. Garnish with watercress and tomato wedges. Makes 4 sandwiches.

A peasant's sandwich for any class.

SARDINE AND EGG ON RYE

4 hard-boiled eggs
1 3¾ oz. can sardines, drained
1 tablespoon mayonnaise
1 green onion, sliced thin
4 large round thin slices rye bread
  butter or margarine

Mash hard-boiled eggs and sardines together. Add mayonnaise and green onions and mix. Add more mayonnaise if necessary to bind eggs and sardines. Butter bread. Divide egg and sardine mixture onto slices of rye bread. Spread evenly. Cut each slice into quarters. Garnish sandwiches with olives, radishes and small gherkins. Makes 4 open face sandwiches.

A fast disappearing still life.

PITA AND EGG

  4 pita breads
  6 hard-boiled eggs, sliced
  8 pieces sweet pickled red peppers
  4 large, thin onion slices
  ½ pint yogurt

Cut tops of pita about one inch from top. Open bread to form a pocket and put in the onion slice flat against one of the sides of each bread. Then laying the pita flat, make layers of the eggs, peppers and yogurt. Eat like a sandwich. Garnish with Greek olives, tomato wedges and radishes. Makes 4 sandwiches.

A pocketful of sandwich.

The World In An Eggshell

DESSERTS

CUSTARDS

Custards are made in many lands under different names but the basic recipe is the same. Milk may become cream in one place or even evaporated milk. Sometimes it can be made with only yolks. Or a combination of whole eggs and yolks. Flavorings vary from any one or combinations of vanilla, cinnamon, nutmeg, brandy, port wine, marsala or rum. The English like to put a whole poached peach in a dish and surround it with custard. The Spanish, French and Portuguese and sometimes the Americans coat the custard in caramel. In Spain, Portugal, Mexico, and South America this custard is called Flan. In France it is called Creme au Caramel. The resourceful Danes merely put brown sugar in the bottom of the custard cup to make its own caramel. The English layer it with cake and wine and call it Trifle. The Italians layer it with cake and rum and call it Zuppa Inglese. The French sprinkle it with brown sugar, broil the custard and call it Creme Brulee. And every firm custard has a version of soft custard to pour on fruit, pudding and cake.

CUSTARD

4 eggs, slightly beaten
½ cup sugar
⅛ teaspoon salt
3 cups milk, scalded
1 teaspoon vanilla
nutmeg

Baked Custard: Mix eggs, sugar and salt. Pour milk into egg mixture, stirring constantly. Add vanilla. Pour into baking dish or custard cups that have been rinsed with cold water. Sprinkle with nutmeg. Set in pan of hot water and bake in a 325 degree oven for 45 minutes or until a knife inserted in the center comes out clean. Cool and chill. Serves 6.

Soft Custard: Combine ingredients listed above with the exception of the vanilla and nutmeg. Cook in a double boiler over simmering water that does not touch the bottom of the pan. When mixture coats the spoon, remove from heat. Add vanilla. Cool and use as a dessert sauce over puddings, cake or fruit. You may also fold whipped cream into the cold custard for a more lavish dessert.

CUSTARD PIE

Bake custard in buttered pie pan. Chill. When pie is cold invert on rack covered with waxed paper. Lay over it a pie shell that has been baked on outside of pan the same size as custard pan. Hold firmly together, invert and—the custard is in the crust.

Soft focus on desserts.

COCONUT CUSTARD PIE

      5 eggs
      ½ cup plus 1 tablespoon sugar
    2½ cups rich milk, scalded
      1 teaspoon vanilla
      1 teaspoon almond extract
      ¼ teaspoon salt
      1 unbaked 9" pie shell
      4 ozs. moist coconut

Beat eggs slightly, add remaining ingredients except coconut, stirring to combine. Sprinkle coconut evenly over pie shell, then pour in custard. Bake in a 450 degree oven 10 minutes, reduce heat to 325 degrees and bake about 25 minutes longer. Cool before serving.

Mack Sennett's favorite pie.

CREME BRULEE

2 cups half and half
4 egg yolks, beaten
   brown sugar

Heat half and half to boiling. Boil for one minute. Remove from fire and slowly pour into beaten egg yolks, stirring constantly. Return to a very low heat and continue beating until it returns to boiling. Pour into a buttered baking dish. Sprinkle with a half inch layer of brown sugar. Place under broiler to carmelize the sugar and form a crust. Cool and then chill. Serves 4.

This is an upper crust dessert.

TRIFLE

½ lb. poundcake, sliced
dry sherry
raspberry jam
soft custard (page 101)
whipped cream
glace fruit

Place the sliced cake in a glass bowl. Pour enough sherry over the cake to thoroughly moisten it. Spread 2 or 3 tablespoons jam over the cake. Chill for several hours. Pour a recipe of chilled soft custard over the cake. Chill for one hour or more. Cover with a layer of stiffly whipped cream and decorate with glacé fruit.

A stiff upper dessert!

ZUPPA INGLESE

½ cup sugar
⅓ cup instant or granular flour
¼ teaspoon salt
2 cups milk, scalded
4 eggs, separated
½ teaspoon vanilla
½ teaspoon orange extract
1 spongecake, rectangle approximately 10″ x 7″
¾ cup dark rum
¼ cup sugar

Combine sugar, flour and salt and gradually add scalded milk and stir until smooth. Beat egg yolks in the top of a double boiler. Add the milk mixture. Stir constantly and cook over hot water until thick. Remove from heat, add flavorings. Cool. Butter a rectangular pan that can go from refrigerator to oven. Split cake in half crosswise. Place a layer of cake in bottom of pan. Drizzle half the rum over it and cover with half of the custard. Repeat with cake, rum and custard. Place in refrigerator. Make a stiff meringue of the egg whites and ¼ cup of sugar. Completely cover cake and custard with meringue up to the edges of the pan. Place in a 300 degree oven until meringue is golden. Chill again. Serve with a large spoon in individual dishes. Serves 6-8.

When the Italians Trifle with the English!

CUSTARD FILLING

½ to ¾ cup sugar
6 tablespoons flour
¼ teaspoon salt
2 cups milk or cream
4 egg yolks, beaten
2 tablespoons butter
1 teaspoon vanilla

Mix dry ingredients thoroughly and add ½ cup cold milk to make smooth paste. Scald remaining milk. Pour flour paste into scalded milk, stirring until mixture thickens. Cover and cook over hot water until thoroughly cooked (about 15 minutes). Remove pan from double boiler. Pour a small amount of sauce into yolks. Pour egg mixture into sauce. Return to double boiler, stir and cook 2 or 3 minutes until egg is thickened. Remove from fire, add butter and vanilla. Cool before using. Use as filling for cream puffs or Boston Cream Pie.

A collector's item.

FLOATING ISLAND

            5 eggs, separated
            1 cup sugar
         2¼ cups half and half
           ⅛ teaspoon salt
            1 teaspoon vanilla

Beat egg whites very stiff gradually adding half of the sugar. Heat the half and half in a skillet and reduce the heat to very low. Drop tablespoons of the meringue into the simmering half and half. Cook for 2 minutes, turn gently with a slotted spoon and cook another 2 minutes. With the slotted spoon remove the meringues from the skillet and place them on a folded towel. Beat the yolks, remaining sugar and salt and pour the warm half and half into the eggs beating constantly. Cook in a double boiler until the mixture coats a spoon. Add vanilla. Pour in a serving bowl. Cool and chill. To serve, arrange the meringues decoratively on the custard. Serves 4-6.

Looks good enough to eat!

ZABAGLIONE

6 egg yolks
6 tablespoons sugar
dash salt
6 tablespoons sweet sherry

Combine egg yolks, sugar, and salt in the upper half of a double boiler. Beat with an electric mixer until blended. Gradually add sherry. Put over hot (not boiling) water and continue beating for 6-7 minutes until thick and fluffy. Serve immediately in dessert glasses. Serves 6.

Made to order Italian dessert.

CHOCOLATE SOUFFLE

    5 eggs, separated
    2 tablespoons flour
    2 tablespoons butter
  ¾ cup milk
    2 squares chocolate, melted
  ½ cup fine dry bread crumbs
  ½ cup sugar
    1 teaspoon vanilla
  ¼ teaspoon salt

Melt butter, add flour and cook for a minute. Gradually add milk, stir constantly until it becomes a thick sauce. Add melted chocolate, bread crumbs and sugar. Add hot mixture slowly to well-beaten egg yolks and beat thoroughly. Add vanilla. Fold mixture into egg whites that have been beaten with salt until stiff. Bake for 45 minutes in a baking dish (buttered on bottom only) set in water in a 350 degree oven. Serve immediately. Serves 6.

A NOW dessert. It doesn't wait for anyone.

CHOCOLATE POTS DE CREME

1 pint plus 2 tablespoons half and half
1 lb. semi-sweet chocolate
6 egg yolks, well beaten

Scald half and half and add chocolate. Stir until chocolate is melted and just about reaches boiling point. Pour over egg yolks. Mix thoroughly and pour into individual pots. If you don't have the French "pots," you may use demi-tasse cups or small dishes. Serves 12.

*A very, very dessert! Very classic. Very French
. . . and very chocolaty.*

CHOCOLATE MOUSSE

8 ozs. semi-sweet chocolate
½ cup sugar
¼ cup strong black coffee
5 eggs, separated
1 teaspoon brandy
  salt

In the top of a double boiler melt chocolate with sugar and coffee. Stir until very smooth. Remove from heat and cool. Add the egg yolks and brandy. Beat egg whites and salt until very stiff and gently fold the chocolate mixture into the whites. Pour into a serving dish or individual dishes. Chill. Serves 6.

A Rococoa dessert.

BREAD AND BUTTER PUDDING

1½ cup currants
   thin sliced bread, buttered
4 eggs
2 tablespoons sugar
¼ teaspoon nutmeg
   pinch cinnamon
2 cups milk

MERINGUE

2 egg whites
   dash salt
4 tablespoons sugar

Scatter some currants in a one quart buttered baking dish. Add a layer of buttered bread. Add more currants, then more bread, alternating the two until all the currants are used. Beat eggs. Add sugar, spices and milk. Beat well and pour over the bread and currants. Let dish stand for about 10 minutes. Place in a pan of hot water and bake for about 45 minutes in a 350 degree oven. Cover with meringue made by beating 2 egg whites with salt and gradually beating in sugar until whites are stiff. Return to oven to brown. Serve warm. Serves 6.

Bread and butter for dessert.　　**113**

LEMON FILLING

¼ cup butter or margarine
1 cup sugar
3 eggs, slightly beaten
grated rind of 1 lemon
6 tablespoons lemon juice
⅛ teaspoon salt

Place butter in pan over hot water to soften. Add remaining ingredients. Cook over simmering water, stirring constantly, until very thick and heavy. Cool and store covered. Makes 1⅓ cups.

A tart filling for filling tarts.

PASHKA

4 hard-boiled egg yolks
1 pint farmer style or small curd cottage cheese
3 egg yolks
1 cup sugar
¼ cup melted butter
½ teaspoon vanilla
3 tablespoons flour
½ cup chopped candied fruit
3 egg whites
blanched almonds

Force hard-boiled egg yolks and cheese through a sieve. Beat thoroughly. Cream egg yolks and sugar and add melted butter. Add to first mixture and beat well. Fold in flour, vanilla and candied fruit. Beat egg whites until stiff and fold in. Pour into a tall, narrow buttered casserole or mold. Place in a pan of hot water and bake in a 325 degree oven for 35-45 minutes. Cool. Unmold. Chill. Decorate with almonds.

Traditional Easter cheese pudding.

VIRGINIA EGG NOG

6 eggs, separated
½ cup sugar
1 cup milk
1 cup bourbon or Southern Comfort
1 cup heavy cream
nutmeg

Beat yolks and sugar until very light. Add milk and whiskey. Beat cream and fold in. Beat whites and fold in. Should be chilled very thoroughly before serving. Sprinkle nutmeg on top when served.

Why wait for Christmas?

EGG NOG

1 egg, separated
2 teaspoons sugar
¼ teaspoon vanilla
1 cup cold milk

Beat egg yolk and 1 teaspoon sugar. Add milk and vanilla, beating thoroughly; pour into tall glass. Beat egg white and remaining sugar until stiff. Pile egg white on top of drink. Makes 1 serving.

An egg nog for minors.

Masterpieces

BAKING

PAVLOVA

4 egg whites
¼ teaspoon salt
½ teaspoon cream of tartar
1 cup powdered sugar.

Beat egg whites with salt and cream of tartar until they are foamy. Gradually add a very small amount of sugar (a scant tablespoon at a time) to whites and keep beating until all the sugar is used and meringue is very stiff. Place a circular piece of white oiled and floured paper in the bottom of a 9″ pie pan. Spread meringue in pan and up the sides of the pan. Bake in a 225 degree oven for one hour. Turn off heat and leave meringue in oven for another hour. Loosen sides with a knife. Turn pan over on a flat surface. Unmold meringue and carefully remove paper. Place right side up on a serving plate. Fill with whipped cream and cover with strawberries or raspberries.

Meringue Down Under.

RHUBARB CUSTARD MERINGUE PIE

3 eggs
1 cup sugar
½ cup milk
½ teaspoon almond extract
1 lb. fresh rhubarb, cut in ½ inch slices
1 9″ baked pie crust
3 egg whites
¼ cup sugar

Beat 3 whole eggs and sugar at medium speed until light lemon colored. Gradually add milk, beating until smooth. Add almond extract. Place rhubarb in bottom of baked pie crust. Pour custard over it. Make a stiff meringue of 3 egg whites and ¼ cup sugar. Spread over pie. Bake in a 350 degree oven for 30 minutes. Cool at room temperature before serving.

How to avoid a rhubarb. Seconds for everybody.

LEMON PIE

6 egg yolks
6 tablespoons lemon juice
1 cup sugar
grated rind of 1 lemon
⅛ teaspoon salt
3 egg whites
1 baked 9" pie shell

MERINGUE

3 egg whites
6 tablespoons sugar
¼ teaspoon salt

Beat yolks, add sugar, lemon juice, rind and salt. Mix thoroughly. Place over hot water and cook until a soft custard is formed. Stir constantly. Cool thoroughly. Fold in 3 stiffly beaten whites and pour into pie shell. Cover with meringue made by beating remaining 3 egg whites with salt until foamy. Add sugar gradually (1 tablespoon at a time) and continue beating until stiff. Place pie in a 350 degree oven for 10-12 minutes or until meringue is lightly browned. Cool. Serves 4-6.

As American as apple pie.

CHRISTMAS PLUM PUDDING

1 lb. dry bread crumbs	1 cup flour
1 pint hot milk	1 teaspoon cinnamon
8 eggs, separated	½ tablespoon cloves
2 cups sugar	1 tablespoon allspice
1 lb. currants	1 tablespoon ginger
1 lb. raisins	½ lb. chopped suet
½ lb. candied fruit, chopped fine	½ cup brandy or
juice of 1 lemon	grape juice

Pour milk over crumbs. Cool. Add egg yolks beaten with sugar. Add fruit mixed with flour and spices, suet, lemon juice, and other liquid. Fold in stiffly beaten whites. Pour batter into a well-buttered 5 cup mold. Cover mold with lid or heavy aluminum foil held in place with string. Place mold on a rack in a deep saucepan. Add an inch of boiling water to saucepan (under the rack). Cover pan. Steam over a low flame for 6 hours. It may be necessary to add a little boiling water to the pan from time to time. To serve, unmold on a platter. Serve warm with hard sauce made by beating together one cup powdered sugar, 4 tablespoons soft butter, dash salt, 1 teaspoon brandy and one egg. Sauce should be chilled before using.

A "Bah humbug" plum pudding. No plums.

ANGEL FOOD CAKE

    1 cup sifted cake flour
  1½ cups sugar
   12 egg whites
   ¾ teaspoon salt
  1½ teaspoons cream of tartar
   ½ teaspoon vanilla
   ½ teaspoon almond extract

Sift ½ cup sugar with flour three times. Beat egg whites to a foam, then sprinkle salt and cream of tartar over surface and continue beating until stiff and glossy. Continue beating, adding the cup of sugar in 2 tablespoon portions. Add flavoring. Sift flour and sugar mixture into meringue in four portions. Fold quickly. Pour into ungreased tube pan 10″ by 4½″. Bake in a 350 degree oven for one hour. Invert pan and cool cake before removing it from pan.

Heavenly inspiration!

YOLK SPONGE CAKE

3 cups sifted flour
3 teaspoons baking powder
12 egg yolks
1 teaspoon salt
2 teaspoons lemon extract
2 cups sugar
1 cup hot water

Sift flour and baking powder together 4 times. Add salt and flavoring to yolks and beat at slow speed until lemon-colored. Alternately add sugar and hot water, beating thoroughly after each addition. Add flour mixture, about one-fourth at a time. Beat thoroughly after each addition. Line a loose bottom 10 by 4¼ inch tube pan with ungreased white paper. Pour batter into pan and bake in a 350 degree oven for one hour. Invert pan and let cake cool before removing it from pan, usually about one hour.

An old world composition.

POPPY SEED CAKE

¾ cup poppy seeds
¾ cup milk
¾ cup butter or margarine
1½ cups sugar

2 cups sifted cake flour
2 teaspoons baking powder
4 egg whites, stiffly beaten

Soak the poppy seeds in milk for 3 hours. Pre-heat oven to 350 degrees. Cream butter and sugar. Sift flour and baking powder together. Alternately add the flour mixture and the poppy seed mixture to the butter and sugar. Beat well after each addition. Fold in the egg whites. Pour the batter into 2 buttered and floured cake pans. Bake for 35 minutes. Remove from oven, cool on racks for 10 minutes. Remove from pans and cool thoroughly. Put custard filling between layers and completely coat the outside of the cake.

CUSTARD FILLING

2 cups milk
1 cup sugar
3 tablespoons cornstarch

salt
4 egg yolks
¼ cup rum

Combine all ingredients. Cook over very low heat in a heavy saucepan until thick. Cool.

An edible sculpture.

FLUFFY FROSTING

1 egg white
1 cup sugar
¼ teaspoon cream of tartar
½ cup boiling water
½ teaspoon vanilla

Combine egg white, sugar and cream of tartar in small bowl of electric mixer. Add boiling water and immediately beat at high speed until very thick and fluffy. The bowl will be filled to top with frosting. Add vanilla. Makes frosting sufficient to frost two 8 or 9 inch layers.

Seven minute frosting made in under two minutes.

KOLACKY

    1 yeast cake
    2 tablespoons warm milk
    ½ teaspoon sugar
    ½ lb. butter or margarine
    3 cups flour
    ½ teaspoon salt
    4 egg yolks
    ½ pint hot sweet cream
    4 tablespoons sugar
      grated rind of a lemon
      jam

Dissolve the yeast in warm milk with ½ teaspoon sugar. Combine butter and flour with salt as for pie dough. Beat egg yolks, add cream, sugar and lemon rind and add to flour-butter mixture together with the raised yeast. Set aside in cold place or refrigerator over night. Roll out to ½ inch thickness. Cut with 2½" cookie cutter. Make a deep dent in the center with your thumb. Fill dent with jam. Let rise in a warm place for 15 minutes. Bake in a 350 degree oven for 20 to 25 minutes. Serve warm.

Coffee and . . .

PATE A CHOUX

½ cup water
¼ cup butter
½ cup sifted flour
⅛ teaspoon salt
 2 eggs

Place butter and water in saucepan, heat to boiling. Add flour and salt. Stir vigorously and cook batter until it leaves sides of pan and forms a ball. Remove from heat. Beat in eggs, one at a time. Drop batter from teaspoon on greased baking sheet about 2 inches apart. Bake in a 425 degree oven for 45 to 50 minutes. Dry in oven about 20 minutes with the heat turned off. Cut off the top portion with a sharp knife. Set top aside. Scoop out any soft insides. Fill with Custard Filling (page 101) and cover with top piece. Refrigerate until ready to serve.

The French confection.

CHOCOLATE CHERRY MERINGUES

2 egg whites
1/4 teaspoon cream of tartar
salt
1 cup powdered sugar
2 tablespoons cocoa
1/2 teaspoon vanilla
24 small pieces red glacé cherries

Beat whites with cream of tartar and salt until they are foamy. Gradually add sugar and beat until very stiff. Add cocoa and vanilla. Line cookie sheet with white paper that has been oiled and floured. Drop rounded spoonfulls of meringue about 2 inches apart on sheet. Put a piece of cherry on each. Bake in a 225 degree oven for one hour. Turn off heat and leave in oven for another hour. Makes 24 kisses.

A wisecrack—no yolk intended!

BERLINKRANZ

    4 hard-boiled egg yolks
    2 cups powdered sugar
    4 egg yolks
    1 lb. butter or margarine
    6 cups flour
    ½ teaspoon almond extract
    ½ teaspoon vanilla
    2 egg whites
      red and green sugar

Mash hard-boiled yolks and cream them with sugar. Add raw
yolks slightly beaten, flavoring, then butter and flour. Chill
dough, mold bits of dough into strips about ½ inch in diameter
and 4 to 5 inches long. Form into rings with ends crossed. Dip
into slightly beaten egg whites, sprinkle with colored sugar.
Bake in a 375 degree oven, 8-10 minutes, or until delicately
browned. Makes about 8 dozen cookies.

Christmas wreath cookies.

FLICKA COOKIES

1 cup butter or margarine
1 cup powdered sugar
½ teaspoon almond extract
6 hard-boiled egg yolks
2 cups flour
½ teaspoon salt
  jelly
  powdered sugar

Cream butter and sugar. Add flavoring. Press yolks through a fine sieve and add to creamed mixture. Work in the flour and salt. Chill. Roll to one-eighth inch thickness. Cut half of dough with a 2 inch cookie cutter and remainder of the dough with the same size doughnut cutter. Bake in a 350 degree oven about 20 minutes or until lightly browned. Spread jelly on solid cookies and cover each with cooky cut with doughnut cutter. Sprinkle with powdered sugar. Makes about 4 dozen cookies.

Cookies in a frame.

INDEX

Angel Food Cake, 124
Apple Pancake, 65
Artichoke Bobatie, 54
Asparagus Pudding, 74

Bacon Cheese Souffle, 23
Berlinkranz, 131
Bread and Butter Pudding, 113
Broiled Eggs, 17

CAKES
  Angel Food, 124
  Poppy Seed, 126
  Yolk Sponge, 125
Carrot Souffle, 78
Cheese Puffs, 38
Cheese Souffle, 63
Chicken Mousseline, 53
Chilis Rellenos, 62
Chocolate Cherry Meringues, 130
Chocolate Mousse, 112
Chocolate Pots de Creme, 111
Chocolate Souffle, 110
Chutney Omelette, 64
Coconut Custard Pie, 103
Coddled Eggs, 1 and 2, 16

COOKIES
  Berlinkranz, 131
  Chocolate Cherry
    Meringues, 130
  Flicka Cookies, 132
Corn-Cheese Escallop, 76
Cream Puffs, 129
Creamed Eggs Montreal, 51
Creme Brulee, 104
Custard, 101
Custard Filling, 107
Custard Pie, 102

CUSTARDS
  Chocolate Pots de Creme, 111
  Coconut Custard Pie, 103
  Creme Brulee, 104
  Custard, 101
  Custard Filling, 107
  Custard Filling for
    Poppy Seed Cake, 126
  Custard Pie, 102
  Floating Island, 108
  Rhubarb Custard
    Meringue Pie, 121
  Trifle, 105
  Zabaglione, 109
  Zuppa Inglese, 106

Denver Sandwich, 92
Deviled Eggs, 37

DUMPLINGS
    Egg Dumplings, 70
    Gnocchi, 69
    Spaetzle, 68

Egg and Caviar Sandwich, 94
Egg and Olive and Bacon
        Sandwich, 95
Egg Dumplings, 70
Egg Flower Soup, 45
Egg Foo Yung, 61
Egg Nog, 117
Egg Nog, Virginia, 116
Egg Salad Sandwiches 1, 2, 3, 88
Egg Salad Aspic, 42
Egg Smorrebrod, 93

EGGS, METHOD OF COOKING
    Broiled, 17
    Coddled 1, 2, 16
    Deviled, 37
    Fried, 12
    Hard-Boiled, 14
    Omelettes, 18
    Poached, 11
    Scrambled, 13
    Shirred, 15
    Soft Boiled 1, 2, 10
Eggs A La King, 52

Eggs and Onions, 24
Eggs Basque, 31
Eggs Benedict, 30
Eggs Bombay, 57
Eggs Shoyu, 26
Escalloped Spinach, 77

Flicka Cookies, 132
Floating Island, 108
Fluffy Frosting, 127
French Toast, 32
Fried Eggs, 12
Fried Mozzarella, 40
Fried Sandwiches, 89
Frito Misto, 75
Frittata, Zucchini, 58

Gnocchi, 69
Golden Cube Garnish
        For Clear Soup, 44

Ham & Egg Cake, 22
Hard-Boiled Eggs, 14
Hash & Eggs, 29
Hollandaise Sauce, 81
Hollandaise, Blender, 83
Hollandaise, Easy, 82
Huevos Lisboa, 27
Huevos Rancheros, 28

Kedgeree, 60
Kolacky, 128

Lemon Filling, 114
Lemon Pie, 122
Lettuce Salad with Cream, 79

Matzo Balls, 71
Matzo Brei, 33
Mayonnaise, 84
Mayonnaise, Blender, 85
Meat Loaf with Hard-
    Boiled Eggs, 59
Monte Cristo Sandwich, 91

Nest Eggs, 48
Noodle Ring, 72

Omelette, 18
Omelette, variations,
    18-19, 56, 64
Onion Cake, 80

Pashka, 115
Pate A Choux, 129
Pavlova, 120
Pickled Eggs, 36
Piquant Dressing, 43

Pita and Egg Sandwich, 97
Plum Pudding, Christmas, 123
Poached Eggs, 11
Poppy Seed Cake, 126
Potato and Onion Omelette, 56
Potato Puffs, 73

Quenelles, 39
Quiche Lorraine, Individual, 41

Rhubarb Custard Meringue
    Pie, 121

Salami and Eggs, 25
Sardine and Egg Sandwich
    on Rye, 96

SAUCES
    Hollandaise, 81
    Hollandaise, Blender, 83
    Hollandaise, Easy, 82
    Mayonnaise, 84
    Mayonnaise, Blender, 85
Scrambled Eggs, 13
Shirred Eggs, 15
Skillet Corn, 55
Soft-Boiled Eggs 1, 2, 10
Souffled Cheese Sandwich, 90

SOUFFLES
   Bacon Cheese Souffle, 23
   Carrot Souffle, 78
   Cheese Souffle, 63
   Chocolate Souffle, 110
Spaetzle, 68
Special Strata, 50
Sponge Cake, 125

Trifle, 105

West Indies Casserole, 49

Yolk Sponge Cake, 125

Zabaglione, 109
Zucchini Frittata, 58
Zuppa Inglese, 106